Golden Spike

*National Historic Site
by Robert M. Utley
and Francis A. Ketterson, Jr.*

*Division of Publications
National Park Service
U.S. Department of the Interior
Washington, D.C., 1969*

For sale by the Superintendent of Documents, U.S. Government Printing Office
Washington, DC 20402

CONTENTS

ORIGIN OF THE PACIFIC RAILROAD	1
Early Sentiment	2
Organization of the Central Pacific	4
Railroad Act of 1862	5
Organization of the Union Pacific	6
Railroad Act of 1864	7
BUILDING THE PACIFIC RAILROAD	11
The Builders	11
The Construction Companies	14
Methods of Construction	16
Progress of the Central Pacific	20
Progress of the Union Pacific	22
THE DASH TO PROMONTORY	27
The Great Railroad Race	27
Climbing the Promontory	30
The Last Month	39
Driving the Last Spike	45
Promontory After May 10, 1869	52
SIGNIFICANCE OF THE PACIFIC RAILROAD	57

When the telegrapher's three dots—DONE—flashed coast to coast from Promontory Summit, Utah, at 12:47 p.m. on May 10, 1869, rails from east to west were joined and the Pacific Railroad had become a reality. It had been long in coming.

Despite virtually unanimous public sentiment for a Pacific Railroad, almost four decades of debate and discussion, liberally dosed with meaningless oratory, preceded the driving of the last spike. Within a matter of months after the introduction of the steam locomotive to the United States in 1830, farsighted men conceived the idea of a railroad from the Atlantic to the Pacific. By mid-century, after a rail network had spread over the East and Midwest to the Mississippi River, a railroad to connect this network with the West Coast became a great public issue. Those who advocated the road saw both its necessity and the immediate benefits it would bring to the Nation. But only a few, and they but vaguely, understood the vast influence a Pacific Railroad would have on the continental development of the United States.

ORIGIN OF THE PACIFIC RAILROAD

In 1850 the U.S. House of Representatives' Committee on Roads and Canals succinctly stated the basic motives of the great segment of public opinion that championed the building of a railroad to the Pacific. Such a road, said the committee, would "cement the commercial, social, and political relations of the East and the West," and would be a "highway over which will pass the commerce of Europe and Asia."

Proponents of a Pacific Railroad based their arguments mainly on its commercial importance. The settlement of the Oregon question in 1846, the discovery of gold in California in 1848, and the admission of California to statehood in 1850 swelled the population of the Pacific Coast. And with commerce almost wholly dependent upon the long, slow journey around Cape Horn or across the Isthmus of Panama, both East and West foresaw a large and lucrative trade speeding by rail across the continent. Even more important, the promoters confidently predicted that a Pacific Railroad would divert much of the trade with Europe and Asia from ship to rail. "The real objective point," recalled U.P. executive Sidney Dillon, "continued to be China and Japan and the Asiatic trade."

The commercial motive remained dominant from first to last, but there were other considerations that carried greater influence with Congress, and led the national lawmakers to overcome the deeply rooted opposition to Government-sponsored internal improvement projects and throw the weight of the United States, both moral and material, behind the idea. The railroad would hasten the final subjugation of the American Indians. It would also enormously reduce the time and expense to the United States in transporting mail and Government supplies. With the outbreak of the Civil War, political bonds between California and the Union had to be strengthened to counter the threat of that State's secession. The war also dramatized the defenseless condition of the Pacific Coast. Rapid transcontinental transportation was a necessary ingredient in solving both problems.

2

From the early days of our Nation's life,
From the time of the first steam train,
Farsighted men had seen the need
Of rails from coast to coast.
Long years of debate: What's the best route?
Surveys of western wilds
From northern plains to deserts south
Four paths for the rails were known.
But the Nation was spinning,
Was tearing,
Dividing.
War!

Early Sentiment

As early as 1832, seven years after the successful run of British engineer George Stephenson's steam locomotive in England, an Ann Arbor, Mich., newspaper, *The Emigrant,* sounded the first call for a railroad to the Pacific. Even earlier, in 1819, John Mills of Virginia had suggested connecting the Atlantic and Pacific Oceans with a "system of steam-propelled carriages." The idea spread, and in 1836 John Plumbe, civil engineer of Dubuque, Iowa, held a public meeting to discuss such a project—the first of uncounted meetings to be called throughout the Nation in the next 25 years.

During the decade of the 1840's the widely publicized western explorations of John C. Frémont and the stirring events of the Mexican War focused attention on the West and helped to popularize the idea of a transcontinental railroad. Equally effective were the promotional activities of Asa Whitney, a New York merchant active in the China trade whose obsession was a railroad to the Pacific. He wrote articles, lectured constantly, and expounded his views to the foremost public figures of the day. He conceived the first definite plan for a road and laid it before Congress with the endorsement of 16 State legislatures and many public conventions and boards of trade across the country.

Although Congress failed to sanction his plan, Whitney had made the Pacific Railroad one of the great public issues of the day. Throughout the 1850's numerous railroad conventions were held at major cities of the East, and one convened at San Francisco. Leading statesmen—John C. Calhoun, Jefferson Davis, Stephen A. Douglas, and others—declared their support. Both the Republican and Democratic Parties wrote the Pacific Railroad into their platforms, although the Democrats, still skeptical of Federal participation in internal improvement, made Government aid contingent on its constitutionality. The project inspired such enthusiasm that Sen. Andrew P. Butler of South Carolina was moved to complain: "It was said of the Nile that it was a god. I think that this Pacific railroad project comes nearer being the subject of deification than anything else I have ever heard of in the Senate. Everyone is trying to show his zeal in worshiping this great road."

Politicians might agree on the necessity for a Pacific Railroad and on the impossibility of constructing one without Federal aid, yet each year legislation introduced in Congress for this purpose came to grief. The lawmakers could not agree on an eastern terminus because the section that captured the terminus would gain immense political and economic benefits. Aside from these considerations, Congressmen knew almost nothing of the comparative merits of the possible routes across the country. To remedy this, they appropriated money in 1853 for the Army's Corps of Topographical Engineers "to ascertain the most practicable and economical route for a railroad from the Mississippi River to the Pacific Ocean."

Between 1853 and 1855 the Engineers surveyed two northern and two southern routes. They discovered that a railroad could be built on any one of the four, although the 32d parallel, along which the Southern Pacific later built, would be the least expensive. This route was, of course, as politically objectionable to Northerners as the northern routes were to Southerners. The Pacific Railway Surveys thus failed to resolve the issue; the principal result was a set of handsomely illustrated volumes that contributed enormously to knowledge of the American West. When the first transcontinental railroad was finally built, it followed none of these four routes.

The failure to agree on a Pacific railroad route was only one aspect of a larger and more important disagreement. By mid-century the people of North and South had grown more firmly entrenched in their sectional views, and compromise, the hallmark of the American political scene, became a word without meaning. In this atmosphere there was no hope for a Pacific railroad, in fact little hope for the Nation to continue as before. The only certainties were debates more acrimonious than the day before. And then—civil war.

The railroad was a national dream.
It wanted a dreamer of action.
A man came forth who found a way
Across the Sierra Nevada.
The dream needed more to give it life,
Needed money to make it move.
Not dreamers now, but men of means
Were found in Sacramento.
The Four could start; that was all.
More was needed yet.
They sent the dreamer to the East,
To the Capitol in Washington City.
Out of the Chaos of Civil War
Came decision for the road.

Organization of the Central Pacific

While Congressmen debated in the immediate pre-war years, a handful of Californians acted. An engineer of the Sacramento Valley Railroad, Theodore D. Judah, became obsessed with the idea of a transcontinental railroad. Like Whitney before him, Judah lobbied with politicians, merchants, and financiers, both in Washington and in his home State. Making little headway, he took to the field in the summer of 1860 to locate a line through the formidable Sierra Nevada. With preliminary data indicating the feasibility of Donner Pass, Judah set out to raise money for the project. San Francisco gave him a cool reception, and he turned to Sacramento.

Here Judah infected four merchants of modest fortune with his enthusiasm. Leland Stanford, Collis P. Huntington, Mark Hopkins, and Charles Crocker were convinced that a transcontinental railroad could be built and that its builders would become rich and famous. But more immediate advantages interested them at the moment. Not only did the prospect of Federal aid appear brighter than ever in the spring of 1861, but immense profits seemed assured to the railroad that tapped the Nevada mining towns burgeoning on the eastern slope of the Sierra. On June 28, 1861, these men incorporated, under State laws, the Central Pacific Railroad Company of California.

As chief engineer of the Central Pacific, Judah went again to the mountains for the summer. In October 1861 he set out once more for Washington, this time with a briefcase full of maps, profiles, and plans.

The Railroad Act of 1862

During the winter of 1861-62, Judah worked tirelessly for legislation to aid the Pacific Railroad. So did a group of eastern promoters who hoped to build west from the Missouri River. President Lincoln, convinced not only of the military benefits of the road but also of its necessity for binding the Pacific Coast to the Union, strongly supported the campaign. With no prospect of a southern route being adopted and with no Southerners to oppose a northern route, Senators and Representatives had little difficulty agreeing on the terms of an acceptable bill. During May and June 1862 such a bill successfully made its way through Congress and on July 1 received the President's signature.

The Railroad Act of 1862 threw the support of the United States Government behind the transcontinental railroad. It authorized the Union Pacific Railroad, the first corporation chartered by the National Government since the Second United States Bank, to build westward from the Missouri River to the California boundary or until it met the Central Pacific. (Congress fixed the longitude and the President named

Omaha the terminus.) The act also empowered the Central Pacific, which already had a charter from California, to push farther east and connect with the Union Pacific.

Government aid took the form of land grants and subsidies. The road was to have a 400-foot right-of-way through the public domain, plus 10 sections of land for every mile of track. These were alternate sections, five out of every 10 on each side of the track, or one-half the land in a belt 20 miles wide. For each mile of track completed, moreover, the companies were to receive 6-percent, 30-year U.S. bonds, principal and interest repayable at maturity, which were to constitute a first mortgage on the railroad. The bond subsidy was fixed at $16,000 a mile east of the Rockies and west of the Sierras, $32,000 a mile between the mountain ranges, and $48,000 a mile in the mountains.

Organization of the Union Pacific

The 1862 Act also named 163 men, 25 of whom constituted a quorum, to form the Board of Commissioners of the Union Pacific Railroad and Telegraph Company. These men were to work out a provisional organization of the company. When $2 million had been subscribed to Union Pacific capital stock and 10 percent of this amount paid in cash to the U.S. Treasury, the provisional officers were to give way to permanent officers.

A quorum of commissioners met at Chicago on September 2, 1862, and elected provisional officers. Within a year the requisite stock had

U.P. engineering survey party in the Wasatch Mountains, 1866.   Union Pacific

been subscribed and 10 percent in cash paid to the Treasury. In October 1863, the stockholders gathered to form a permanent organization. They chose 30 directors, and elected officers: Maj. Gen. John A. Dix, president; Thomas C. Durant, vice president; Henry V. Poor, secretary; and John J. Cisco, treasurer. General Dix never took office, and until 1869 Vice President Durant guided the affairs of the Union Pacific.

With blare of bands the work began,
Long speeches stirred the crowd.
But lack of three things prevented speed:
No men, no iron, no gold.
War was still upon the land,
Hungry for the three.
Progress was slow, or not at all;
The railroad could not move.
Congress acted to help the road,
Made possible its building.
The means were soon to be at hand,
The race would soon begin.

The Railroad Act of 1864

Impressive ceremonies—more impressive than those 6 years later at the driving of the last spike—launched the two railroads. The Central Pacific broke ground at Sacramento on January 8, 1863, the Union Pacific at Omaha on December 2, 1863.

Neither road made much progress. The war sent the price of materials soaring and made labor extremely scarce. Capital could not be enlisted, for war prosperity afforded better investment opportunities than in a railroad whose first dividend lay far in the future. In California the Central Pacific found itself bitterly opposed by a powerful alliance of stage, ship, freight, and telegraph companies that fought with every weapon at its command. As California's Republican war Governor, however, Leland Stanford managed to bring some State financial aid to his company. With this, and by borrowing on their personal security, the four associates pushed their rails 18 miles east of Sacramento by February 1864. But the Union Pacific did not even lay its first rail until the spring of 1865. The railroad builders, facing ruin, turned again to Congress with quite valid reasons for more Government help. The Railroad Act of 1864 was the result.

Signed by the President on July 2, 1864, this act doubled the resources made available to the railroad by the parent legislation. Although reducing the right-of-way from 400 to 200 feet, the 1864 Act doubled the land grant. The companies were now to receive 20 sections of land per mile—10 alternate sections on each side of the track. Of more immediate benefit, the Government relinquished its first lien on the railroad by authorizing the companies, as they received Government subsidy bonds, to issue equal amounts of their own 6-percent, 30-year bonds. The company bonds were now to constitute a first mortgage on the road, the U.S. bonds a second mortgage on the road. In addition to these major concessions, the act contained a number of minor liberalities that made compliance with Government regulations far easier than before.

The act limited the Central Pacific to building no more than 150 miles east of the California-Nevada boundary. Of this provision, Collis P. Huntington later wrote: "150 miles ought not to have gone into the bill; but I said to Mr. Union Pacific, when I saw it, I would take that out as soon as I wanted it out." When he did, 2 years later, he fired the starting gun for the great railroad race.

The 1864 Act made the United States "virtually an endorser of the company's bonds for the full amount of its own subsidy," and now both the U.P. and the C.P. could draw on double the amount of subsidy granted for each mile of completed road. "The financial problem has been solved," rejoiced Stanford in July 1865, "and the result is abundant financial means to press forward the work to its utmost development." To abundant finances, the end of the Civil War added abundant labor and material. The two companies marshalled forces for a 10-year job that would take less than 4 years. □

BUILDING THE PACIFIC RAILROAD

The Pacific Railroad had been the subject of discussion, debate, and oratory for so many years that, once construction actually began, it aroused the most intense interest and curiosity throughout the Nation. Few people dreamed in 1865 that there would ever be more than one railroad across the continent. The expense, almost everyone agreed, would prohibit other roads. Newspapers all over the country therefore followed the progress of the road in infinite detail, and it was described in expansive terms as the eighth wonder of the world and "the great work of modern America." From 1865 to 1869 the Pacific Railroad dominated the national consciousness as did few other events.

These were the men who built the road:
Great men, small men,
Names known, names unknown.
Faces in history.
These were the men:
Men from the East, men from the West,
Audacious men, audacious times.

The Builders

The men who built the Pacific Railroad rank among the most dynamic, brilliant, and resourceful of the 19th century. The key figures in each company were well versed in management and in construction, fields requiring different talents, involving different work, and attracting different temperaments. Working sometimes together, sometimes in opposition, they pushed the Pacific Railroad to completion against almost insurmountable obstacles, both financial and engineering.

Composing the management of the two companies were men skilled in corporate finance and administration. Their methods were those of the 1860's, employed by most of their contemporaries in business—practices condemned as thoroughly unethical by today's standards. Thus the truly great achievement of these men has been tarnished by the judgment of a later generation. They were, in fact, the first victims of the revulsion against such methods that swept the country during the early 1870's.

The Big Four ran the Central Pacific. Leland Stanford served as president and handled all matters requiring State and local political influence and manipulation. Collis P. Huntington, vice president, made his headquarters in New York. He negotiated for purchases of equipment and materials, solicited investment from Eastern and European capitalists, and represented the company in Washington. Treasurer Mark Hopkins—quiet, meticulous, and clear-minded—balanced the flamboyant Stanford and Huntington. He exerted great influence over his associates and usually saw the solution to difficult problems. Forceful and energetic, Charles Crocker was a silent partner in the management, earning his principal fame as the fieldman who supervised construction of the road.

Dominant in the Union Pacific management were Thomas C. Durant and Oakes Ames. Durant was vice president of the railroad, and, until 1867, president of the Crédit Mobilier of America, the construction company that built the road. A man of tireless energy and hair trigger temper, he made enemies of almost everyone with whom he

Stanford University

Gov. Leland Stanford

Southern Pacific

Collis P. Huntington

Southern Pacific

Mark Hopkins

worked. Yet on the management level, he, more than anyone, was responsible for completion of the Union Pacific. Ames, Boston shovel manufacturer and Congressman from Massachusetts, came to the aid of the company in its blackest financial crisis. His vast resources kept construction going, although in the end personal bankruptcy resulted.

A bitter quarrel between Durant and Ames burdened the Union Pacific management. Durant, a speculator, wanted to make a fortune from construction and then abandon the road. Ames, the investor, was interested in building a good road as a long-term investment. Aggravated by other differences and by a personality clash, the Durant-Ames feud influenced the management of the U.P. throughout most of the construction period.

Other men of importance were Sidney Dillon, who succeeded Durant as president of the Crédit Mobilier and later became president of the Union Pacific; John Duff, director; and Oliver Ames, brother of Oakes Ames and General Dix's successor as president.

Both railroads had capable men in the field. With the exception of Crocker, they kept largely aloof from financial and organizational problems, devoting themselves entirely to building the railroad. As a consequence, they escaped the public condemnation that later fell upon the managers of the companies.

Charles S. Crocker — Southern Pacific

Oakes Ames — Library of Congress

T. C. Durant — Union Pacific

For the Central Pacific, Crocker, as president of the construction company, was the driving power. Crocker summed up his role: "Why, I used to go up and down that road in my car like a mad bull, stopping along wherever there was anything amiss, and raising Old Nick with the boys that were not up to time." Crocker's right-hand man was his construction superintendent, James H. Strobridge. Chief Engineer Samuel S. Montague (Judah, so instrumental in forming the Central Pacific, had died in 1863) carried the surveys across Nevada and Utah to Green River, Wyo., and directed all engineering work from Sacramento to Promontory. His chief assistant was Lewis M. Clement.

The Union Pacific also had an able corps of fieldmen. Chief Engineer Grenville M. Dodge supervised U.P. surveys to the California border. Samuel B. Reed served as superintendent of construction. The partnership of John S. and Dan T. Casement held the contract for tracklaying and much of the grading. These were the men who carried the rails from Omaha to Promontory—1,085 miles, in 4 years.

The Construction Companies

Both the Union Pacific and the Central Pacific met the same basic financial difficulty. Government bonds provided only half the necessary capital, and the land grants, potentially of enormous value, supplied no ready cash. Thus construction depended heavily upon private investment. But there was no incentive to investors. A railroad through virtually uninhabited country could not be expected to return a dividend for many years. And Congress required railroad securities to be sold at par for cash. Both companies therefore resorted to a favorite device of 19th-century railroad builders—a construction company with interlocking directorate free of Government regulation.

The Union Pacific's construction company was the Crédit Mobilier of America. In 1864 Durant bought the Pennsylvania Fiscal Agency, a corporation loosely chartered by the Pennsylvania Legislature to engage in practically any kind of business, and renamed it the Crédit Mobilier. The directors and principal stockholders of this company were virtually the same as those of the Union Pacific. Greatly simplified, the process worked like this: The Union Pacific awarded construction contracts to dummy individuals, who in turn assigned them to the Crédit Mobilier. The Union Pacific paid the Crédit Mobilier by check (i.e., cash, for the benefit of Congress), with which the Crédit Mobilier purchased from the Union Pacific, at par, U.P. stocks and bonds, which it then sold on the open market for what they would bring. The construction contracts were written to cover the Crédit Mobilier's loss on the securities and to return generous profits. In this manner the directors and principal stockholders of the Union Pacific, in their opposite role as directors and stockholders of the Crédit Mobilier, reaped large profits as the rails advanced.

The Big Four used an almost identical device to build the Central Pacific. Although in practice continuing to share in the management of the Central Pacific, Crocker resigned from the directorate and formed the construction firm of Charles Crocker and Company, in which Stanford, Hopkins, and Huntington were the only stockholders. The connection between the two companies was too obvious, and in 1867 the Big Four organized the Contract and Finance Company, with Crocker as president. Acting for the Central Pacific, they awarded to this company the contract for building the road from the California line to the junction with the Union Pacific, as well as for supplying all materials, equipment, rolling stock, and buildings. The chief advantage of the Contract and Finance Company over the Crédit Mobilier, as railroad historian Robert E. Riegel pointed out, "was that it was able to get its accounts into such shape that no one has ever been quite able to disentangle them."

Such techniques not only pushed the railroad to completion in record time, but also made its financiers extremely wealthy men. The Union Pacific cost about $63.5 million to build, of which about half represented the Government's loan. The best estimate of profits gained is about $16.5 million, although the enormity of this figure emerges only when it is understood that at no one time did invested capital exceed $10 million. Profits thus amounted, not to 27½ percent, but to more than 200 percent. The Central Pacific's figures are more difficult to arrive at, mainly because many of its books were "accidentally" destroyed by fire during the Congressional investigation of the Crédit Mobilier. The best authority, however, places the cost of construction at $36 million. The company received land grants and Government bonds valued at $38.5 million, while Stanford admitted that $54 million in Central Pacific stock transferred to the Contract and Finance Company in payment of construction contracts represented virtually net profit.

There was an inevitable reckoning. Both railroads were burdened with inflated capitalization that meant decades of high rates and operating losses. The Crédit Mobilier investigation in 1872, moreover, brought the railroads bad publicity that strained relations with the public and the Government for many years and produced hostile legislation. Nevertheless, almost all railroad historians, while deploring the financial buccaneering of the Pacific Railroad builders, agree that only through such methods could the railroad have been built without far more liberal Government aid.

Methods of Construction

Sordid though the financial history of the Pacific Railroad may be, it is more than balanced by the dramatic construction story, in which the fieldmen of the two companies justly took pride. By completing the railroad across a 1,775-mile wilderness in less than 4 years, they set a record yet unequaled.

Both companies dealt with tremendous logistical problems. At great expense the Central Pacific had to ship by sea all equipment, tools, rolling stock, rails, bolts, and fishplates from the Atlantic Coast around Cape Horn or across the Isthmus of Panama to San Francisco. The Union Pacific, until completion of the Chicago and Northwestern to

Central Pacific's depot at Truckee   *Stanford University*

Council Bluffs in November 1867, shipped its materials and supplies to Omaha by Missouri River steamers or by wagon. Even ties, which the C.P. obtained in profusion from the Sierra, the U.P. had to import until its line reached the Black Hills of Wyoming and the Wasatch Mountains. All material, plus supplies for the army of workers, then had to be forwarded by train from the terminus to end-of-track, a transportation requirement that grew heavier with each mile the rails advanced. And beyond end-of-track the grading crews and surveying parties had to be supplied by wagon train.

During the first years, scarcity of labor delayed construction. For the Union Pacific, the end of the Civil War solved this problem. Veterans of the Union armies, mostly Irish immigrants, flocked to Omaha to enlist in Casement's grading and track gangs. The Central Pacific, however, in distant California, could not draw on this formidable labor pool. Railroad wages failed to tempt men who could earn more at the mines and perhaps, with luck, make a fortune. Strikes plagued the builders. Once, in order to break a strike, Crocker sent for some Chinese workers. They turned out to be excellent workers, and soon the Big Four were sending ships to China for recruits. By 1865 there were 7,000 Chinese, by 1868, 11,000. "Crocker's pets" they were called, and to them the word of "Mistuh Clockee" was law. Stanford later asserted that "Without them it would have been impossible to complete the western portion of this great National highway."

Despite differences in financing the tracklaying and grading, the basic field organization for accomplishing the work was the same for both roads. Far in advance, staking the route, ranged the surveying parties—

Southern Pacific   Chinese at work on the Central Pacific

engineers, rodmen, flagmen, chainmen, axmen, teamsters, herders, and, in Indian country, a cavalry escort. They ran preliminary surveys, followed by actual location surveys. Next came the graders. Usually they prepared 100 miles of grade at a time—on the plains in about 30 days. In the mountains it took much longer, and here the graders worked as much as 200 to 300 miles in advance of the track. Bridge, culvert, and trestle crews usually worked 5 to 20 miles from the railhead. The graders used pick and shovel for earth work, wheelbarrow and horse- or mule-drawn wagons for earth movement. For blasting cuts and tunnels through rock, they experimented with liquid nitroglycerine, but, for the most part, they used enormous quantities of black powder.

Behind the graders came the tracklayers. This phase of work excited the greatest interest among spectators. A correspondent from the East described it on the Union Pacific:

> A light car, drawn by a single horse, gallops up to the front with its load of rails. Two men seize the end of the rail and start forward, the rest of the gang taking hold by twos, until it is clear of the car. They come forward at a run. At the word of command the rail is dropped in its place, right side up with care, while the same process goes on at the other

Bear River City, Wyo., typical of the "hell-on-wheels" towns that followed the U.P. acros

side of the car. Less than thirty seconds to a rail for each gang, and so four rails go down to the minute. . . . The moment the car is empty it is tipped over on the side of the track to let the next loaded car pass it, and then it is tipped back again; and it is a sight to see it go flying back for another load, propelled by a horse at full gallop at the end of 60 or 80 feet of rope, ridden by a young Jehu, who drives furiously. Close behind the first gang come the gaugers, spikers, and bolters, and a lively time they make of it. It is a grand "anvil chorus". . . . It is in triple time, three strokes to the spike. There are 10 spikes to a rail, 400 rails to a mile, 1,800 miles to San Francisco—21,000,000 times are those sledges to be swung; 21,000,000 times are they to come down with their sharp punctuation before the great work of modern America is complete.

At or near end-of-track was the base camp. It consisted of construction headquarters, tents for housing the army of workers, and acres of materials and supplies to support work at the front. As rails advanced 100 to 200 miles, the camp moved forward to a new location. Adjacent to each camp along the line of the Union Pacific a tent city sprang up almost overnight. Some survived after the camp departed, while others died as quickly as they had been born. The U.P. left a trail of these towns across the country: Frémont, Kearney, North Platte, Julesburg, Sidney, Cheyenne, Laramie, Benton, Green River, Evanston, and Promontory. Until the camp moved, they were roaring centers of fun-making and frequent homicides. The population consisted

Union Pacific

chiefly of gamblers, whiskey-peddlers, prostitutes, and criminals of every variety. Together they relieved the Irishmen of most of their wages.

By contrast, the Central Pacific failed to give birth to the "hell on wheels" that characterized the Union Pacific railhead. The docile Chinese did not drink and gambled only among themselves, hence were poor material for parasites looking for easy money. Also, while the Missouri River frontier produced every type of adventurer eager to seek his fortune in the West, Californians had already come west and were content to remain. Crocker and Strobridge, moreover, imposed law and order on their towns and kept liquor and vice under a watchful control.

This was the land they had to cross:
Sierra Nevada, Rockies' slopes,
Plains, deserts, basins.
Land of the Indians.
The land has little changed its face:
Mountains as rugged, plains as wide,
Deserts dry as a century ago.
Only the Indians changed.

Progress of the Central Pacific

Although the Central Pacific laid its first rail more than a year before the Union Pacific, it encountered its toughest work—the crossing of the

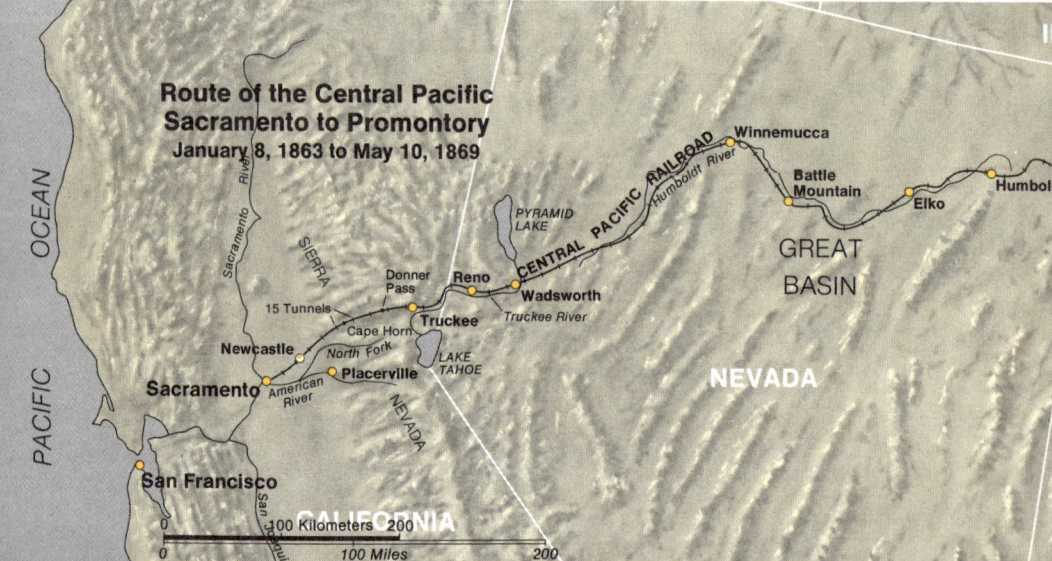

Sierra Nevada—almost immediately. The rails reached Newcastle, 31 miles from Sacramento, on June 4, 1864. For the next 4 years, with numerous delays produced by financial, political, topographical, and weather problems, the C.P. labored to surmount the Sierra. The mountains presented enormous engineering obstacles to overcome in the face of severe weather. Deep fills, rock cuts, high trestles, snaking grades, and 15 tunnels totaling 6,213 feet through solid granite proved necessary. To protect the track from snowslides, 37 miles of wooden snowsheds and galleries had to be built.

Recalling some of the difficulties, Construction Superintendent Strobridge testified:

During the winter of 1866 and 1867 and the following winter of 1867 and 1868 there were unusually heavy snowfalls in the upper Sierra Nevadas. . . . The tunnels were got under way with as large a force as could be used on them and the remainder of the force was sent to the Truckee Canyon on the east slope of the Sierras, where the snowfall was not so great as to entirely prevent grading during the winter, the total force being about 13,500 men at this time. The snow was so deep that it was impossible to keep the tunnel approaches clear and we were compelled to make tunnels through the snow from the dump to the tunnel entrances. Snow tunnels were also required to get into camp. In many instances our camps were carried away by snowslides, and men were buried and many of them were not found until the snow melted the next summer. In the spring of each year the men were taken back from the Truckee into the mountains and an average depth of ten or twelve feet of snow was cleared away before grading could be commenced.

The total snowfall of the season was about forty feet, and the depth of hard, settled snow in midwinter was eighteen feet on a level in Summit Valley and Donner Pass, over which we hauled on sleds track material for forty miles of railroad, three locomotives, and forty cars from Cisco

to Donner Lake, where all was reloaded on wagons and hauled over miry roads to Truckee, a total distance of twenty-eight miles, at enormous cost. [Thus] the road was forced to the east slope of the Sierra Nevadas. . . .

The line was opened to Clipper Gap, 43 miles from Sacramento, on June 10, 1865; to Colfax, 55 miles, on September 10; to Dutch Flat, 68 miles, in July 1866, and to Cisco, 94 miles, on November 9. Here end-of-track remained while thousands of coolies blasted in the Summit Tunnel. The tunnel was 1,659 feet long, and, during the year that work on it stopped end-of-track, other crews toiled at grading and track-laying on the east slope. After completion of the tunnel in August 1867 the gap quickly closed, and the first train steamed into Truckee on April 3, 1868. The tracks reached Reno, Nev., 154 miles from Sacramento, on June 10, 1865, and Wadsworth, 189 miles, on July 22.

The Central Pacific had put the roughest part of the job behind it. Ahead lay the Nevada desert and conditions were favorable for rapid progress. Even so, the Union Pacific was far advanced. In May 1868 it had reached Laramie, Wyo., 537 miles west of Omaha. It had laid 348 more miles of track than C.P., but ahead lay the Wyoming Black Hills and, across the Wyoming Basin, the Wasatch Mountains.

Progress of the Union Pacific

From Omaha up the Platte Valley to the Wyoming Black Hills, the Union Pacific had easy going. The level valley of the Platte River presented few engineering problems. While the Central Pacific struggled in the Sierra, the Union Pacific's grade and track advanced steadily and smoothly.

The Union Pacific followed the old Oregon Trail up Nebraska's Platte Valley. It did not, however, cross the Continental Divide at famous South Pass. In 1865, still in uniform and campaigning against hostile Indians, General Dodge had accidentally discovered what he thought might be a practicable pass across the Wyoming Black Hills. Examination of this pass by U.P. surveyors confirmed Dodge's suspicions. Through Wyoming, therefore, the Union Pacific kept south of the Platte and the Sweetwater, thus considerably shortening the route.

But the Union Pacific faced an obstacle that never troubled the Central Pacific, and in Nebraska it appeared in its ugliest form. The Sioux and Cheyenne Indians possessed a strength and a will to resist that the Paiutes of Nevada had long since lost. As the U.P. invaded their country, the dullest native soon understood what the rails meant to the Indian way of life. War parties swept down on surveyors, graders, and tracklayers, then vanished before pursuit could be organized. Appreciating the importance of the railroad to their own task of destroying the Indian barrier, Generals Grant and Sherman stripped the frontier of troops to place large forces on the line of the Union Pacific. Forts sprang up along the right-of-way—McPherson, Sedgewick, Morgan, D. A. Russell, and Sanders. Soldiers guarded the construction workers and rode with the surveyors.

In the Wyoming Basin, where the road penetrated Sioux country, the surveying parties, with their small cavalry escorts, bore the brunt of Indian hostility. One tragedy occurred in June 1867, when Sioux

warriors attacked Assistant Engineer Percy T. Browne and eight cavalrymen. Forting up on a knoll, Browne and his men held the Indians at bay until dusk, when Browne caught a bullet in the stomach. The warriors withdrew during the night, and the soldiers carried Browne on a blanket litter 15 miles to LaClede Station of the Overland Stage Company. There he died.

On August 6, 1867, with railhead far out in Wyoming, Indians struck near Plum Creek, Nebr. (present-day Lexington). Chief Turkey Leg's Cheyennes descended on the railroad and, as one of the Indians later recalled, "we got a big stick, and just before sundown one day tied it to the rails and sat down to watch and see what would happen." First came a handcar, which struck the "big stick" and sent its passengers flying. The Indians killed them, except for a man named Thompson, who was scalped but did not die. (A warrior dropped the scalp and Thompson retrieved it. Later, recovering from his wounds, he tried unsuccessfully to grow it back in place. For years it was on display in a jar of alcohol at the Council Bluffs Public Library.) Delighted with their first success, the Cheyennes next pried up some rails. A freight train came along, ran off the track, and piled up, a mass of flames, in a ravine next to the roadbed. Another train, following the first, quickly reversed itself and backed out of the danger area. The Indians broke into the freight cars and had a grand party with the contents—barrels of whiskey, bolts of calico, ribbons, bonnets, boots, and hats. All the following day they indulged in an orgy of fun-making, like children set free in a toy store. Finally, just as the raiders were leaving, a train loaded with Maj. Frank North's battalion of Pawnee Indian scouts steamed up to the wreck and hastened the departure.

In the Black Hills the Union Pacific encountered its first difficult country and began to draw $48,000 a mile in subsidy bonds. Here, also, smoldering personal animosities within the U.P. hierarchy reached a crisis in the summer of 1868. Consulting Engineer Silas Seymour, Vice President Durant's man at the front, changed and lengthened a location that Dodge had accepted. Durant came west to support Seymour, and probably to try forcing Dodge's resignation. At a tense conference at Fort Sanders, Wyo., a shaky truce was reached. Dodge would be allowed to locate the line of the road without further interference from Seymour. Also present at the conference were Ulysses S. Grant, who was touring the West as part of his presidential campaign, Generals William T. Sherman and Philip H. Sheridan, who were accompanying Grant through this part of the country, and an array of lesser civil and military notables.

The Union Pacific kept its stride. In 1865 it graded and bridged 100 miles and laid 40 miles of track. In 1866 it completed 265 miles of road; in 1867, 245 miles; and in 1868, 350 miles. In the winter of 1868-69 the rails moved into the rugged Wasatch Mountains where, on the summit and in Weber and Echo Canyons, the U.P. experienced on a lesser scale something of the ordeal that the C.P. had endured in the Sierra.

Surveying parties of both railroads pushed into the Great Salt Lake Basin. Brigham Young, powerful president of the Mormon Church, expected the rails to come through Salt Lake City. But a route around the north end of Great Salt Lake possessed decided advantages, besides avoiding the treacherous salt flats west of the city. The Union Pacific chose to turn north at Ogden and follow the north shore of the lake, bypassing the Utah capital. Young was furious, and he threatened to withhold the Mormon aid on which the U.P. had counted. However, when he discovered that the C.P. had also settled upon the northern route, he accepted the decision and threw the support of the church to both the Union Pacific and the Central Pacific, meanwhile organizing his own Utah Central Railroad to connect Salt Lake City with Ogden.□

Grenville M. Dodge

Gen. U. S. Grant and party at Fort Sanders, 1868.

Union Pacific

THE DASH TO PROMONTORY

It seems to have been the intent of Congress throughout that the two companies should build until they met, then, wherever this might be, join their rails and form a continuous line from the Missouri River to the Pacific Coast. But at each step in the evolution of Pacific Railroad legislation, Congress found it impossible to frame the statutes with sufficient precision to prevent the companies from interpreting them to serve their own purposes. Both companies had very cogent reasons for wishing to build and operate as large a share of the Pacific Railroad as possible. And they were willing to pay a very high price to attain this goal.

The race is on!
The starter's gun has fired.
Spurs dig in the racers' sides,
They run for all or nothing.
One prize, the far Great Basin.
One Spur, the greed for trade.
Another prize: The Nation's eyes
Would fix upon the winner!
The longer line to junction point
Would gain the greater honor.

The Great Railroad Race

Although the loose language of national lawmakers made possible the great railroad race, it was motivated by practical considerations far removed from the halls of Congress. Every mile of track, of course, brought its reward in subsidy bonds and land grants. But there were other compelling reasons for speed. Above all, both companies aimed for Ogden and Salt Lake City, for the railroad that captured these Mormon cities would control the traffic of the Great Basin. If the Central Pacific won, it would carry the trade of the Great Basin over its tracks to San Francisco; if the Union Pacific won, this commerce would flow east to the Mississippi. Each contender, therefore, strained to reach Ogden and shut the other out of the Great Basin.

Each company, moreover, bore a constantly mounting interest on the Government loan and on its own securities. Although the 1864 Act gave them until 1875 to finish the road, every day that tied up capital in construction without the offsetting returns of operation made the burden of interest heavier. The Central Pacific faced the hard reality that the line over the Sierra Nevada had been expensive to build and would be expensive to maintain and operate. Without a compensating mileage on the level country of Nevada and Utah, the railroad would be unprofitable. Finally, the surge of public interest that focused on the Pacific Railroad provided a less tangible but no less powerful incentive. Both companies were convinced that the one that built the greatest length of railroad would enjoy the greatest prestige in the eyes of the Nation.

The Railroad Act of 1866, produced largely by the lobbying of Collis P. Huntington, cleared the way for the race. It restored the provisions of the 1862 Act by authorizing the Central Pacific to "locate, construct, and continue their road eastward, in a continuous completed line, until they shall meet and connect with the Union Pacific Railroad." This act did not specify where the point of junction would be, and from president down to spikers and gaugers, the men of the U.P. and the C.P. set out to advance that point as far into the territory of their competitor as possible.

Two provisions in the acts of 1864 and 1866 helped. One permitted the companies to grade 300 miles ahead of end-of-track. The other permitted them, upon completion of acceptable grade, to draw two-thirds of the Government subsidy bonds before the track had been laid.

As soon as Congress passed the 1866 Act, Chief Engineer Montague sent C.P. surveyors to run lines north of Great Salt Lake and east of Ogden in the Wasatch Mountains. By the spring of 1868 they were working next to the flags of the U.P. survey near Fort Bridger, Wyo. Union Pacific surveyors, meanwhile, had staked out a line across Utah and Nevada to the California border.

During 1868 and 1869, the decisive years of rivalry, both companies put grading crews far ahead of track; the Union Pacific even leapfrogged some graders as far west as Humboldt Wells, Nev. In June

1868 Leland Stanford took the stage to Salt Lake City. During the next 6 months he contracted with Brigham Young and other prominent Mormons to grade the line of the C.P. from the vicinity of Humboldt Wells to Ogden, Utah, a distance of about 200 miles. The U.P. had already let a $2 million grading contract to Young for work between Echo Summit and Promontory Summit.

Thus Mormon crews worked on parallel grades, deriving considerable profit from the rivalry and perhaps a measure of satisfaction at the discomfiture of the companies that had bypassed Salt Lake City. In the final reckoning, the Union Pacific and Central Pacific spent about $1 million on grade that was never used. Also, since the U.P. in the end could meet only half of its financial obligation to the Mormons, Brigham Young obtained $600,000 in U.P. rolling stock to equip his own Utah Central Railroad.

By the end of 1868 the Union Pacific had finished grading to the mouth of Weber Canyon and was laying rails down Echo Canyon. The Central Pacific, its track still in eastern Nevada, had made good progress on grading between Monument Point and Ogden. Both companies forged ahead. Expense was a secondary consideration. The important thing was to reach Ogden first.

In October the Central Pacific had worked a clever stratagem which came very near succeeding. It had filed with the Interior Department maps and profiles of its proposed line from Monument Point to Echo Sunmmit. Secretary of the Interior Orville H. Browning, who had been hostile to the Union Pacific throughout, accepted the documents. Stanford then proceeded on the theory that the Central Pacific line was the true line of the Pacific Railroad, and the only one on which subsidy bonds could be issued. In Washington, Huntington filed application for an advance of $2.4 million in subsidy bonds, two-thirds of the amount due for this portion of the line.

The Union Pacific, of course, protested mightily. Dodge and the Ames brothers hurried to Washington and used all their influence to block the move of the Central Pacific. Browning retreated and in January 1869 appointed a special commission, headed by Maj. Gen. Gouverneur K. Warren, to go west and determine the best route through the disputed territory. Congressmen friendly to the Union

Pacific exacted a pledge from Secretary of the Treasury Hugh McCulloch that he would not issue the bonds until the commission had reported the results of its investigation.

They failed, however, to take account of Huntington's powers of persuasion. As the administration of President Andrew Johnson drew to a close, the Treasury Department prepared the bonds for issue. By March 4, 1869, when Ulysses S. Grant took office as President, it had turned over $1.4 million to Huntington. When the Warren Commission reached Utah, it found that the Union Pacific was almost to Ogden and had obviously won the race. The commissioners therefore confined their investigation to the line between the two railheads. But the issue was to be resolved in Washington, where the new President and the officials of both railroads had been brought by events to appreciate the necessity of working out a compromise.

Dodge and several others interested in the Union Pacific met with Huntington in Washington on April 9, 1869. They drew up an agreement "for the purpose of settling all existing controversies between the Central Pacific and Union Pacific Railroad Companies." The agreement gave both railroads access to the Great Basin, with the terminus to be located west of Ogden at a point to be agreed upon by both companies. The U.P., however, was to build west from Ogden to Promontory Summit and there unite with the C.P. Then it was to sell this segment of the line to Central Pacific. Subsidy bonds were to be issued to the Union Pacific as far as the terminus near Ogden, and to the Central Pacific from the terminus west. The following day, April 10, Congress by joint resolution put its stamp of approval on the agreement.

Climbing the Promontory

To Leland Stanford, in Salt Lake City, it became more and more apparent as 1868 drew to a close that the Union Pacific would reach Ogden first. At this time the Big Four still hoped that Huntington's maneuvers in Washington would checkmate their opponents. But Secretary Browning's vacillation, culminating in the appointment of the Warren Commission in January 1869, made this hope increasingly bleak. "I tell you Hopkins the thought makes me feel like a dog," wrote Stanford, looking at the darkening picture. "I have no pleasure in the thought of railroad. It is mortification."

Toward the Summit from East and West
The rails reached forth to meet.
Between the builders on the plains
Loomed Promontory's bulk.
No easy job that eastern face,
Yet twice the job was done.
Not from need, not only greed,
A race for racing's sake.
Stone to blast, ravines to fill,
Trestles to complete.
Ten miles for five to climb the slope,
The final sprint was on.

Stanford had already turned his attention to the country west of Ogden, rather than the Wasatch Mountains, as the area where the contest would be decided. By occupying and defending the line from Monument Point to Ogden, the Central Pacific might yet gain enough bargaining strength to get into Ogden too, or at least to block the Union Pacific from moving west of Ogden.

The first 48 miles west of Ogden offered no construction problems. The line crossed a level sagebrush plain skirting mudflats north of Bear River Bay. But between Blue Creek and Monument Point stood the Promontory Mountains, a rugged landmass extending 35 miles south into the Great Salt Lake and ending at Promontory Point. A practicable pass separated the Promontory Mountains from the North Promontory Mountains. The summit of this pass lay in a circular basin at 4,900 feet elevation, about 700 feet above the level of the lake. On the west the ascent could be made in 16 relatively easy miles; but on the east, where the slope was more abrupt, the ascent required, for an airline distance of 5 miles from Blue Creek to the summit, 10 tortuous miles of grade with a climb of 80 feet to the mile. Between Monument Point and Blue Creek the Central Pacific and Union Pacific attacked the last stretch of difficult country. Here sheer momentum and public encouragement carried them to the finish line of the great railroad race, even though it had been called off, a draw, in Washington a month earlier.

Stanford had turned his attention to the Promontory on November 9, 1868. He had a long talk with Brigham Young, who at length agreed to furnish Mormon labor for grading the Central Pacific line from Monument Point to Ogden, and promised, in allocating forces, to give preference to neither the U.P. nor the C.P. With Young's backing, Stanford had no difficulty contracting for this work with the firm of Benson, Farr and West, which was headed by Mormon bishops. The contract called for Mormon gangs to prepare the line for track under the supervision of C.P. engineers.

The Union Pacific was calling in its crews from Humboldt Wells, Nev., in order to work west of Ogden. Stanford promptly sent a gang of graders to the Promontory to take possession of strategic points. Then, in mid-November, he went there himself. With Lewis M. Clement, whom Montague had put in charge at the Promontory, and Consulting Engineer George Gray, Stanford carefully inspected the preliminary line run by Butler Ives in 1867. This line, he found, required an 800-foot tunnel through solid limestone. It would cost $75,000 to blast and, moreover, delay tracklaying at a critical time. Stanford ordered his surveyors to stake out a new line at the expense of alinement in order to avoid tunneling. Even so, a fill of 10,000 yards of earth (later famous as the "Big Fill") would be necessary, and rock cuts would consume 1,500 kegs of black powder.

By the end of the year the Central Pacific was well in control of

Laying track on the Union Pacific Railroad.

the line from Monument Point to Ogden. It had men on the entire line. About two-thirds of the grade in each consecutive 20 miles had been finished. Blasting and filling at the Promontory, however, moved slowly. The contractors gave many excuses, but Stanford "started Brigham after them," and they began to work faster. Nevertheless, Stanford believed that Strobridge and the Chinese would have to put the finishing touches on the grade.

As late as mid-January the Union Pacific still had no graders west of Ogden, although its surveyors were running lines parallel to the Central Pacific grade. Stanford lamented on January 15 that:

> From Ogden to Bear River the lines are generally 500 feet to a quarter of a mile apart. At one point they are probably within two hundred feet. From Bear River to the Promontory the U.P. are close to us and cross us twice, on the Promontory itself they will be very close to us, but they have so many lines, some crossing us and some running within a few feet of us and no work on any, that I cannot tell you exactly how the two lines will be. They are still surveying there for a location.

In February the Union Pacific finally put crews west of Ogden. By early March its grade was nearly completed to the eastern base of the Promontory. In mid-March the Mormon company of Sharp and Young, under contract to the Union Pacific, began blasting at the Promontory. Stanford complained on March 14 that, "The U.P. have changed their line so as to cross us five times with unequal grades between Bear River and the Promontory. They have done this purposely as there was no necessity for so doing." But, he said, "we shall serve notice for them not to interfere with our line and rest there for the present."

Union Pacific

During March 1869 both companies went to work on the Promontory with a vengeance. A letter to a Salt Lake newspaper recalls the scene vividly:

> Five miles west of Brigham City on this side of Bear River, is situated the new town of Corinne, built of canvas and board shanties. . . .
>
> Work is being vigorously prosecuted . . . both lines running near each other and occasionally crossing. Both companies have their pile driver at work where the lines cross the river. From Corinne west thirty miles, the grading camps present the appearance of a mighty army. As far as the eye can reach are to be seen almost a continuous line of tents, wagons and men.
>
> Junction City, twenty-one miles west of Corinne, is the largest and most lively of any of the new towns in this vicinity. Built in the valley near where the lines commence the ascent of the Promontory, it is nearly surrounded by grading camps, Benson, Farr and West's headquarters a mile or two south west. The heaviest work on the Promontory is within a few miles of headquarters. Sharp and Young's [Union Pacific] blasters are jarring the earth every few minutes with their glycerine and powder, lifting whole ledges of limestone rock from their long resting places, hurling them hundreds of feet in the air and scattering them around for a half mile in every direction. . . . At Carlisle's [Carmichael's] works a few days ago four men were preparing a blast by filling a large crevice in a ledge with powder. After pouring in the powder they undertook to work it down with iron bars, the bars striking the rocks caused an explosion; one of the men was blown two or three hundred feet in the air, breaking every bone in his body, the other three men were terribly burnt and wounded with flying stones.
>
> . . . there is considerable opposition between the two railroad companies, both lines run near each other, so near that in one place the U.P. are taking a four feet cut out of the C.P. fill to finish their grade, leaving the C.P. to fill the cut thus made. . . .
>
> The two companies' blasters work very near each other, and when Sharp & Young's men first began work the C.P. would give them no warning when they fired their fuse. Jim Livingston, Sharp's able foreman, said nothing but went to work and loaded a point of rock with nitro-glycerine, and without saying anything to the C.P. "let her rip." The explosion was terrific . . . and the foreman of the C.P. came down to confer with Mr. Livingston about the necessity of each party notifying the other when ready for a blast. The matter was speedily arranged to the satisfaction of both parties.
>
> The C.P. have about two-thirds of their heavy work done at this place, while the U.P. have just got under good headway. In other places the grade of the U.P. is finished and the C.P. just beginning, so taking it "all in all" it is hard to say which company is ahead with the work. . . .

The companies encountered the heaviest work on the east slope of the Promontory. Grades of each company, ascending the slope side by side, went down within a stone's throw of each other. They snaked up the face of the mountain, blasting through projecting abutments of limestone, and crossing deep ravines on earth fills and trestles. At the crest they broke through a final ledge of rock to enter the basin of Promontory Summit. The last mile, across the level floor of the basin, required little more than scraping.

Of unfailing interest to observers were the Central Pacific's "Big Fill" and the Union Pacific's "Big Trestle," which crossed a deep gorge about halfway up the east slope. Central Pacific began work on the Big Fill, which Stanford had predicted would require 10,000 yards of dirt, early in February 1869 and was almost finished when a reporter visited the scene in mid-April:

> A marked feature of this work . . . is the fill on Messrs. Farr and West's . . . contract. Within its light-colored sand face of 170 feet depth, eastern slope, by some 500 feet length of grade, reposes the labor of 250 teams and 500 men for nearly the past two months. On this work are a great many of the sturdy [Mormon] yoemanry of Cache County. Messrs. William Fisher and William C. Lewis, of Richmond, are the present supervisors. Our esteemed friend, Bishop Merrill, preceded them. On either side of this immense fill the blasters are at work in the hardest of black lime-rock, opening cuts from 20 to 30 feet in depth. The proximity of the earth-work and blasting to each other, at these and other points along the Promontory line, requires the utmost care and vigilance on the part of all concerned, else serious if not fatal, consequences would be of frequent occurrence. Three mules were recently killed by a single blast.

The Big Trestle was of even greater interest than the Big Fill. The Union Pacific lacked the time to fill in the deep gorge as the Central Pacific had done. Union Pacific therefore decided to bridge the defile with a temporary trestle, which could later, after the roads had joined, be replaced with an earth fill. On March 28, with the Big Fill still under construction, they ordered work begun on the Big Trestle. Situated about 150 yards east of and parallel to the Big Fill, it also required deep cuts at each end.

Finally completed on May 5, the Big Trestle was about 400 feet long and 85 feet high. To one reporter, nothing he could write "would convey an idea of the flimsy character of that structure. The cross pieces are jointed in the most clumsy manner. It looks rather like the 'false work' which has to be put up during the construction of such works. . . . The Central Pacific have a fine, solid embankment alongside it, which ought to be used as the track." Another correspondent predicted that it "will shake the nerves of the stoutest hearts of railroad travellers when they see what a few feet of round timbers and seven-inch spikes are expected to uphold a train in motion."

U.P.'s locomotive No. 119 chugs across the Big Trestle in May 1869

Meanwhile, the rails came forward steadily and rapidly. The Union Pacific entered Ogden on March 8, 1869. By March 15 it was at Hot Springs; by March 23 at Willard City. On April 7 the first train steamed across the newly completed Bear River bridge and entered Corinne. At the same time the Central Pacific was still about 15 miles west of Monument Point. Two days later, on April 9, Dodge and Huntington worked out their compromise in Washington. The U.P. grading crews received orders on April 11 to stop all work west of Promontory Summit. Three days later Stanford ordered all work on the C.P. halted east of Blue Creek, on the eastern base of the Promontory.

The agreement removed all cause for continued competition in grading and tracking. But competition had become a habit, and each company strained to reach Promontory Summit, the agreed meeting-place, before the other. The Union Pacific had won the race to Ogden, but the heavy work on the east slope of the Promontory prevented its winning the race to the Summit. And now, ironically, the U.P. was, in effect, a contractor for the C.P. Its gangs worked with the knowledge that the line from Ogden to Promontory Summit would, according to the Dodge-Huntington agreement, be turned over to the Central Pacific.

The race was in the final stretch,
The oceans soon would join.
No more months of heartbreak toil
To get from coast to coast.
Black powder's blast, maul striking spike,
The music of an epic.
The final movement neared its end,
A symphony in iron.
A mile a day, then three, then eight,
The rails leaped 'cross the land,
As each road tried to best its foe,
To top its rival's deed.
From Eire and the Orient,
Came men to win the honors.
Ten miles of track in one day's work;
Just four more to the finish.

The Last Month

As the two railheads drew closer to each other, an air of excitement pervaded the construction camps north of Great Salt Lake, as well as the rest of the country, which followed the daily progress of the tracklaying in the newspapers. The Central Pacific dismissed its contractors during the first week of April and pushed its Chinese crews forward to finish the grades on the Promontory. The Union Pacific rushed Irishmen to the front to help the Mormon contractors finish the heavy work on the east slope. By April 16 the U.P. and the C.P. tracks were only 50 miles apart. The Union Pacific, moving west across the sagebrush plain from Corinne, slowed for want of ties. The Central Pacific had reached Monument Point and, one-quarter of a mile from the lakeshore, established a sprawling grading camp. Housing the Chinese workers, it consisted of three separate canvas cities totaling 275 tents.

There were constant reminders of the approaching revolution in transcontinental travel. Trains of Russell, Majors, and Waddell freight wagons periodically passed the construction crews. Wells Fargo stagecoaches, which had once spanned the continent, now provided service between the railheads. The run of the coaches daily grew shorter as the rails moved forward 3 to 4 miles a day. For the Army, changes of station between East and West had once meant exhausting marches of several months duration across the western territories. In April 1869 the 12th Infantry, destined for the Presidio of San Francisco, detrained at Corinne and in 2 days marched to the Central Pacific railhead, where the soldiers boarded the train for the coast.

As April drew to a close, officials of the two companies fixed Saturday, May 8, as the date for the ceremony uniting the rails. By the 27th the Union Pacific railhead approached Blue Creek, 10 miles east of the Summit. But rock cuts and three trestles required another 12 to 15 days of labor, even though Reed, in order to break through by May 8, worked his Mormons and Irishmen night and day. While blasters tore at Carmichael's Cut, 1¾ miles above the unfinished Big Trestle, workmen built another trestle at the cut's west entrance. A third trestle spanned Blue Creek. Stanford went to the Union Pacific railhead and offered to let the U.P. run its track across the C.P.'s Big Fill, but found no one with authority to change the line.

Earlier, the Union Pacific had laid 8 miles of track in 1 day—a feat, they boasted, that the Central Pacific had not accomplished. Crocker vowed to top this record, but he cannily waited until the distance between railheads was so short that the U.P. could not retaliate. On April 27, with the Central Pacific 16 miles from the Summit and the Union Pacific, 9, Crocker set out to lay 10 miles of rail in 1 day. But a work train jumped the track after 2 miles had been completed, and he decided to wait until the next day.

At 7:15 a.m., on April 28, with men and supplies carefully massed for the attempt, and with Casement, Reed, and other U.P. officials as witnesses, Crocker gave the signal to start. At once, eight Irish tracklayers supported by an army of Chinese coolies set to work to top the Union Pacific record. The correspondent of the San Francisco *Evening Bulletin* vividly described the activity:

> Each of the four front men ran thirty feet with one hundred and twenty-five tons. Each of the other four men lifted and placed one hundred and twenty tons at their end of the rails. The distance travelled was over ten miles, besides extra walking . . . . Those eight men would not consent to shift, and are proud of their work. They, like all Central Pacific men, are water-drinkers.
>
> Immediately in front of the eight are three pioneers, who, with shovel and by hand, set the ties thrown by the front teams in position; while this is doing, another party are distributing spikes and fresh bolts at each end of the rail, while some of the party are regulating the gauge. These tracklayers are a splendid force, and have been settled and drilled until they move like machinery. . . .
>
> Beside the tracklayers come the spike-starters, who place all the spikes needed in position; then comes a reverend-looking old gentleman who packs the rails and uses the line, and, by motion of his hands, directs the track-straighteners. The next men to the spike-drivers are the bolt screwers, quite a large force. Behind them come the tampers, four hundred strong, with shovels and crow-bars. They level the track by raising or lowering the ends of the ties, and shovel in enough ballast to hold them firm. When they leave it, the line is fit for trains running twenty-five miles an hour. When all the iron thrown on the track has been laid, the handcars run to the extreme front, and the locomotive and iron train come as close to the front as possible; another two miles of iron is thrown off, and the process repeated. Alongside of the moving force are teams hauling tools, and water-wagons, and Chinamen, with pails strung over their shoulders, moving among the men with water and tea. . . .
>
> The scene is a most animated one. From the first pioneer to the last tamper, perhaps two miles, there is a thin line of 1,000 men advancing a mile an hour; the iron cars, with their living and iron freight, running up and down; mounted men galloping backward and forward. Far in the

rear are trains of material, with four or five locomotives, and their water-tanks and cars . . . . Keeping pace with the track-layers was the telegraph construction party, hauling out, and hanging, and insulating the wire, and when the train of offices and houses stood still, connection was made with the operator's office, and the business of the road transacted . . . .

By 1:30 p.m. the track had advanced 6 miles in 6 hours and 15 minutes. The remaining 4 miles could easily be laid. The C.P. crews knew that victory had been won, and Crocker stopped the work for lunch. The site, named Camp Victory, later became the station of Rozel. After an hour of rest the workers returned to the task. By 7 p.m. they had completed more than 10 miles of track, thus topping the U.P., and a locomotive ran the entire distance in 40 minutes to prove to U.P observers that the work was well done.

April 28 carried the Central Pacific railhead to within 4 miles of the Summit. With the Union Pacific still at Blue Creek, Eicholtz ordered iron and ties hauled to the Summit. On May 1 U.P. crews began putting in a sidetrack at the Summit, where tents already announced the birth of the town of Promontory. This same day the C.P. brought its rails to the Summit, 690 miles from Sacramento, the end of the line.

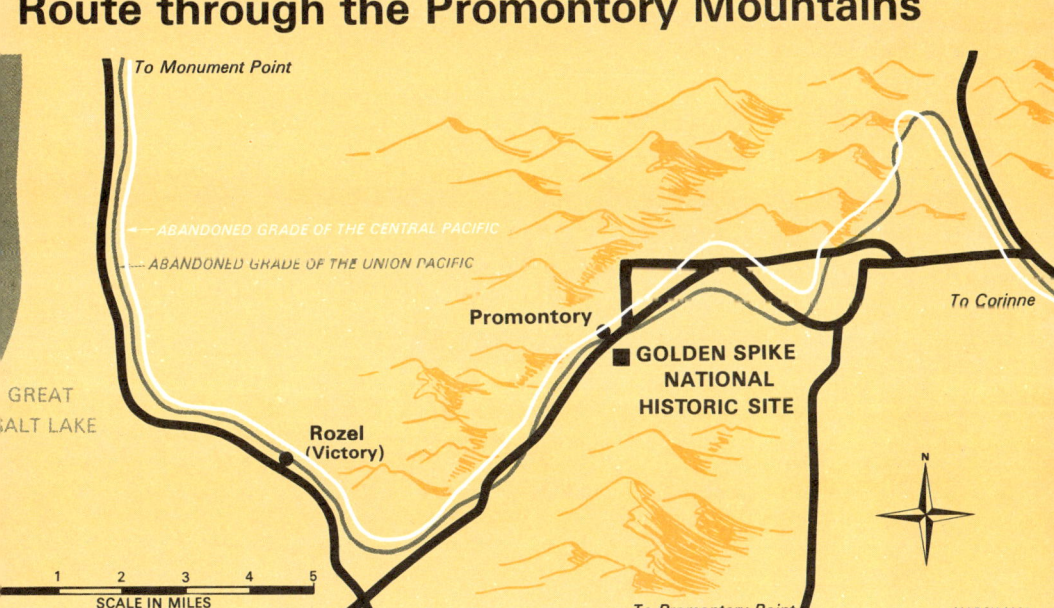

During the first few days of May the population at the Promontory reached its maximum. C.P. camps stretched all the way from Promontory to Monument Point, while U.P. camps dotted the valley of the Summit and cluttered the plain at the foot of the east slope. They bore such names as Deadfall, Murder Gulch, Last Chance, and Painted Post. Jack Casement's headquarters train stood on a siding one-half mile east of Blue Creek bridge. A 68,000-gallon tank, fed by pipes leading to a spring in the hills, had been built at this siding to furnish the camps with water.

The Union Pacific camps here rocked with the riotous living that had characterized their predecessors all the way from Omaha. Noted a reporter from San Francisco:

> The loose population that has followed up the track-layers of the Union Pacific is turbulent and rascally. Several shooting scrapes have occurred among them lately. Last night [April 27] a whiskey-seller and a gambler had a fracas, in which the "sport" shot the whiskey dealer, and the friends of the latter shot the gambler. Nobody knows what will become of these riff-raff when the tracks meet, but they are lively enough now and carry off their share of the plunder from the working men.

Jack Casement Camp Victory

Stanford University

Nor was all peace and quiet in the Central Pacific camps, although the California papers delighted in emphasizing the low moral tone of the Union Pacific. At Camp Victory on May 6, the Chinese clans of See Yup and Yung Wo, whose rivalry stemmed from political differences in the old country, got into an altercation over $15 due one group from the other. The dispute grew heated and soon involved several hundred laborers. "At a given signal," reported a correspondent, "both parties sailed in, armed with every conceivable weapon. Spades were handled, and crowbars, spikes, picks, and infernal machines were hurled between the ranks of the contestants." When shooting broke out, Strobridge and his foreman intervened to halt the fracas. The score, aside from a multiplicity of cuts, bruises, and sore heads, totaled one Yung Wo combatant mortally wounded.

Irish graders of the Union Pacific, on the other side of the Promontory, heard about the battle between the Chinese clans. They decided to have some fun themselves. Next day a gang of them showed up at Promontory, where a Chinese camp had been laid out, and announced their intention "to clean out the Chinese." Fortunately, the inhabitants of this camp were absent on a gravel train, and the Irishmen left without accomplishing their purpose.

Both companies had already recognized that they had more men on the Promontory than the amount of remaining work could keep occupied. Beginning on May 3, therefore, they began discharging large numbers of men and sending others to the rear to work on parts of track that had been hastily laid. "The two opposing armies . . . are melting away," reported the *Alta California,* "and the white camps which dotted every brown hillside and every shady glen . . . are being broken up and abandoned." Riding out from Salt Lake City, photographer Charles R. Savage saw this breakup in progress and wrote in his diary: "At Blue River [Creek] the returning 'democrats' so-called were being piled upon the cars in every stage of drunkenness. Every ranch or tent has whiskey for sale. Verily, men earn their money like horses and spend it like asses."

On May 5 the Union Pacific finally achieved the breakthrough. The last spike went into the Big Trestle and the rails moved out onto the frightening span. A train loaded with iron steamed across it. That evening the final blast exploded in Carmichael's Cut. On May 6 the trestle between Carmichael's Cut and Clark's Cut was finished. The graders went through both cuts, made a swing around the head of a ravine, and passed though a final cut to link up the grade already laid in the basin of the Summit. Here rails and ties had been arranged for rapid tracklaying and, at the Summit itself, a 2,500-foot sidetrack installed.

The Central Pacific waited patiently—May 8 was still the date for joining the rails—as the Union Pacific tracklayers followed closely on the heels of the graders. Late in the afternoon of May 7 the tracklayers came within 2,500 feet of the C.P.'s end-of-track at the Summit. Here they connected, by a switch, with the sidetrack built earlier. Using this sidetrack, the Union Pacific's No. 60, with Casement aboard, came to a halt opposite the Central Pacific railhead, about 100 feet to the southeast of it, and let off steam. The Central's "Whirlwind" rested on its own track. The engineer greeted the Union's

Waiting for the last rails to be laid at Promontory, May 10, 1869.   *Union Pacific*

locomotive with a sharp whistle. "The first meeting of locomotives from Atlantic and Pacific took place."

Only 2,500 feet remained. The next day, May 8, the final drama was supposed to be enacted, but the Union Pacific could not meet the schedule. The last spike was not driven until May 10.

They joined the rails from East and West.
They drove the Golden Spike.
They marked the day with wine and cheers,
And then they signalled "Done."
A railroad built in record time.
The builders justly proud.
They bound the land with bands of iron,
Began the frontier's end.

Driving the Last Spike

At Promontory the afternoon of May 7 was sultry and the sky heavy with rain clouds, which annoyed the photographers trying to capture the climactic scenes of construction. The Stanford Special arrived with an array of dignitaries from California and Nevada headed by Leland Stanford.

Also aboard were the ceremonial trappings to be used in uniting the rails. There was a golden spike presented by David Hewes, San Francisco construction magnate. Intrinsically worth $350, it was engraved with the names of the C.P. Directors, sentiments appropriate to the occasion, and, on the head, the notation "The Last Spike." There was another gold spike, presented by the San Francisco *News Letter;* a silver spike brought by U.S. Commissioner J. W. Haines as Nevada's contribution; and a spike of iron, silver, and gold brought by Gov. A. P. K. Safford to represent Arizona. (Arizonians knew nothing of it. Safford had not yet taken office and had never been in Arizona.) Finally, there was a sliver-plated sledge presented by the Pacific Union Express Company, and a polished laurel tie presented by West Evans, the Central Pacific's tie contractor.

The festive mood of the Stanford Special noticeably dampened when Jack Casement broke the news that the Union Pacific could not hold the ceremony on May 8, as planned, and would not be ready until

May 10. The Stanford party faced the prospect of spending the weekend on the bleak Promontory. To make matters worse, rain began falling. It continued for 2 days, turning Promontory Summit into a sea of mud. Stanford wired the unwelcome news to San Francisco, but too late. The citizens there had already started celebrating. Undismayed, they celebrated for 3 days.

Casement's explanation for the delay was that the trains bringing the dignitaries from the East had been held up in Weber Canyon. Heavy rains had made the roadbed soft and had washed out a trestle. But there was another reason, too. The special train carrying Vice President Durant, Sidney Dillon, and other U.P. officials had reached Piedmont, Wyo., on May 6. A gang of 500 workers surrounded Durant's private car shouting demands for back wages. When the conductor tried to move the train out of the station, the men uncoupled Durant's car, shunted it onto a siding, and chained the wheels to the rails. Here he would stay, they said, until their pay was forthcoming. To make sure, they also took possession of the telegraph office. Durant submitted, wired Oliver Ames in Boston for the money, and paid off the strikers. He was released and managed to be at Promontory on May 10, although the severe headache he suffered that day may well have owed its origin to the experience at Piedmont.

Left in the role of host at Promontory, Casement made up an excursion train, stocked with "a bountiful collation and oceans of champagne," to take the Stanford party sightseeing. The train left Promontory Saturday morning. At Taylor's Mill the Union Pacific staged a "splendid luncheon" on the banks of the Weber River. "The most cordial harmony and good feeling marked their entertainment and all the toasts were drank with loud applause," reported a correspondent. From here the party went to Ogden, rode a short distance up Weber Canyon, and spent the night in Ogden. Next day, Sunday, they returned to Promontory, boarded the Stanford Special, and pulled back to Monument Point to enjoy a repast of plover.

This same day, May 9, Casement's workers at Promontory kept busy. As the rain continued, they laid the final 2,500 feet of track, leaving a length of one rail separating their track from that of the

Central Pacific. They also installed a Y for the locomotives to use in turning around.

The rain ended during the night and May 10 dawned bright, clear, and a bit chilly. During the morning two trains from the East and two from the West arrived at Promontory bearing railroad officials, guests, and spectators. With the construction workers and assorted denizens of Promontory, the crowd totaled, according to the best estimates, 500 to 600 people—far short of the 30,000 that had been predicted.

Among those representing the Central Pacific were Stanford, Strobridge, Montague, and Gray; for the Union Pacific, Durant, Dillon, Duff, Dodge, Reed, and the Casement brothers. Important guests had come from Nevada, California, Utah and Wyoming. Huntington, Hopkins, and Crocker, of the C.P. did not attend; nor did the U.P.'s Oakes and Oliver Ames. Brigham Young sent Bishop John Sharp to represent the Mormon Church. About 15 reporters covered the proceedings. A battalion of the 21st Infantry under Maj. Milton Cogswell, enroute to the Presidio of San Francisco, was opportunely on hand to lend a military air. The military band from Fort Douglas and the 10th Ward Band from Salt Lake City supplied the music.

Officials of both roads had been unable to agree on details of the program. Stanford had come equipped with spikes and other ceremonial trappings, but Dodge wanted the Union Pacific to stage its own last spike ceremony. Only two preparations had been made in advance. The speeches had been written and handed to newsmen in Ogden on Sunday, and the telegraphers had devised an apparatus for transmitting the blows on the last spike by telegraph to the waiting Nation. An ordinary sledge (not the silver-plated one) had been connected by wire to the Union Pacific telegraph line, and an ordinary spike had been similarly connected to the Central Pacific wire. Five minutes before noon, when the proceedings were to begin, Stanford and Durant agreed on a joint program.

The crowd had grown loud and unmanageable, which interfered with the ceremony and made it impossible for most people to see what was happening. One reporter wrote that "it is to be regretted that no arrangements were made for surrounding the work with a line of some sort, in which case all might have witnessed the work without difficulty.

The joining of the rails at Promontory, May 10, 1869. Shaking hands in center are chie

ngineers Samuel S. Montague of C.P. and Grenville M. Dodge of U.P.

As it was, the crowd pushed upon the workmen so closely that less than twenty persons saw the affair entirely, while none of the reporters were able to hear all that was said." This explains the confusion that has surrounded the history of the event.

At noon the infantrymen lined up on the west side of the tracks, and Casement tried, with little success, to get the crowd to move back so that everyone could see. The Union Pacific's No. 119, with Engineer Sam Bradford, and the Central Pacific's "Jupiter," with Engineer George Booth, steamed up and stopped, facing each other across the gap in the rails. Spectators swarmed over both locomotives trying to obtain a better view. At 12:20 p.m. Strobridge and Reed carried the polished laurel tie and placed it in position. Auger holes had been carefully bored in the proper places for seating the ceremonial spikes. Officials and prominent guests formed a semicircle on the east side of the tracks.

Edgar Mills, a Sacramento businessman, served as master of ceremonies and introduced the Rev. Dr. John Todd of Pittsfield, Mass., correspondent for the Boston *Congregationalist* and the New York *Evangelist*. Dr. Todd opened the ceremony with a 2-minute prayer, while telegraph operators from Atlantic to Pacific cleared the wires for the momentous clicks from Promontory. At 12:40 p.m., W. N. Shilling, a telegraph key on a small table in front of him, tapped out: "We have got done praying. The spike is about to be presented."

Next, Dr. W. H. Harkness of Sacramento presented to Durant, with

Central Pacific's "Jupiter" *Southern Pacific*

appropriate remarks, the two gold spikes. Durant slid them into the holes in the laurel tie, and Dodge made the response. U.S. Commissioner F. A. Tritle and Governor Safford presented the Nevada and Arizona spikes, and these Stanford slid into the holes prepared. L. W. Coe, President of Pacific Union Express Company, presented Stanford with the silver sledge, which was then used symbolically to "drive" the precious spikes, although the blows, if indeed any were given, were not sharp enough to leave marks on the spikes.

Finally came the actual driving of the last spike—an ordinary iron spike driven with an ordinary sledge into an ordinary tie. Using the wired sledge, Stanford and Durant both swung at the wired spike. Both missed, to the delight of the crowd. Shilling, however, clicked three dots over the wires at exactly 12:47 p.m., triggering celebrations at every major city in the country. With an unwired sledge, Strobridge and Reed divided the task of actually driving the last spike in the Pacific Railroad.

Amid cheers, the two engineers advanced the pilots of their locomotives over the junction. Men on the pilots joined hands, and a bottle of champagne was broken over the laurel tie as christening. The chief engineers of the railroad shook hands as the photographers exposed wet plates. The military officers and their wives gave the precious spikes ceremonial taps with the tangs of their sword hilts. The Central Pacific's "Jupiter" backed up and the Union Pacific's No. 119 crossed the junction. Then No. 119 backed up and let

Union Pacific   Union Pacific's No. 119

"Jupiter" cross the junction, thus symbolizing the inauguration of transcontinental rail travel.

Shilling sent off two telegrams: "General U. S. Grant, President of the U.S., Washington, D.C. Sir: We have the honor to report the last rail laid and the last spike driven. The Pacific Railroad is finished." "To the Associated Press: The last rail is laid, the last spike driven, the Pacific railroad is completed. Point of Junction, ten hundred eighty-six miles west of the Missouri river and six hundred ninety miles east of Sacramento—Leland Stanford, Thomas C. Durant."

The ceremony over, the precious spikes and tie were removed. Even so, souvenir hunters made necessary numerous replacements of the "last spike" and the "last tie." Central Pacific's "Jupiter" soon left for Sacramento, but Union Pacific's No. 119 remained until evening, presenting, as one reporter observed, "a scene of merriment in which Officers, Directors, Track Superintendents and Editors joined with the utmost enthusiasm." It was late when the celebration ended.

They drove the Spike and then they left.
The armies marched away.
A town grew up, a sickly thing,
Of gamblers, bars, and "doves."
For half a year the changing point,
And then it slowly died.

Promontory After May 10, 1869

Promontory had enjoyed its hour of glory, but the town did not immediately die. The two companies did not agree on a price for the Promontory-Ogden section until November 1869. For nearly a year Promontory served as the terminus, where passengers transferred from one railroad to the other. Union Pacific trains turned around on the Y that had been installed on May 9, while Central Pacific trains used a turntable built shortly before the rails were joined on May 10.

During the months that it served as the terminus, Promontory resembled the other boomtowns that had followed the Union Pacific across the country. A string of boxcars on a siding provided offices and living quarters for railroad employees. A row of tents, many with false board fronts, faced the railroad across a single dirt street. They housed hotels, lunch counters, saloons, gambling dens, a few stores and shops, and the nests of the "soiled doves." Signs advertised such alcoholic potations as "Red Cloud," "Red Jacket," and "Blue Run." Liquor sales boomed. Water was scarce. The nearest source was 6 miles away, and the railroads were forced to haul long strings of tank cars full of water to Promontory from springs 30 to 50 miles distant.

A large number of "hard cases" descended on Promontory, including, reported the correspondent of the Sacramento *Bee,* "Behind-the-Rock Johnny, hero of at least five murders and unnumbered robberies." Three-card monte, ten-die, strap game, chuck-a-luck, faro, and keno flourished in the gambling tents. A gang of cutthroat gamblers and confidence men called the "Promontory Boys" set up headquarters and were "thicker than hypocrites at a camp meeting of frogs after a shower." Their *modus operandi* was to put "cappers" aboard the trains at Kelton or Corinne to gain the confidence of passengers. At Promontory the cappers led their victims to one of the gambling tents and into the clutches of the Promontory Boys.

Promontory's life as a "hell on wheels" boomtown was a short but lively one. J. H. Beadle, editor of the *Utah Daily Reporter,* summed up its character when he wrote: "4,900 feet above sea level, though theologically speaking, if we interpret scripture literally, it ought to have been 49,000 feet below that level; for it certainly was, for its size, morally nearest to the infernal regions of any town on the road."

The trestles on the Union Pacific line ascending the east slope of the Promontory continued to be a source of concern. A Government inspector, Isaac N. Morris, in May 1869 reported to President Grant on this part of the line, grudgingly approving all except the trestles.

For a mile and a half [going east from Promontory] the ties . . . are virtually laid on the ground, but the road then passes through several sand-banks, some comparatively small and some of formidable proportions, with intervening spaces of nearly level surface; thence it passes through rock excavations, one being some forty feet deep and a quarter of a mile long through the heaviest body of the mountain, overlooking Salt Lake; thence it sweeps around the mountain's side to its base, describing in its course a succession of short curves, so sharp indeed that an ascending and descending train would collide before either would be aware of the proximity of the other. I measured the width of the cuts, and found them so nearly in compliance with the standard of construction that they may be so regarded. Before reaching the descending curve running on the side of the mountain, two dells or ravines are crossed on trestle-work, one as nearly as I could judge . . . about two hundred and fifty feet long and thirty feet deep. These trestle-structures, unknown to the law, but familiar to the line of the road, and one over Blue Creek, not far distant, are very frail and dangerous. It is the purpose of the company, I was told, to fill up these ravines so as to have a solid road bed over them. The sooner this is done the better for the safety of lives and property. . . .

After the Central Pacific took over the line from Promontory to the terminus near Ogden, it eliminated the two trestles on the slope. The company did this apparently sometime during 1870 by laying track on its own grade, installed during the great railroad race. Thus the new line followed the C.P. grade from somewhere near the eastern base of the Promontory, across the Big Fill parallel to the Big Trestle, across another fill parallel to the trestle connecting Carmichael's and Clark's Cuts, and thence in a sweep to the north across the valley to the Summit.

With transfer of the terminus to Ogden in early 1870, the lusty days of Promontory came to an end. The Central Pacific, however, built a station, water tank, and roundhouse at Promontory. Locomotives pulling heavy trains required additional power to climb the east slope, and the company kept helper-engines at the summit for this purpose. The town also became headquarters of a railroad cattle enterprise, and the company built the "Crocker Mansion" about 1 mile to the northwest. With eight bedrooms and as many bathrooms, it was a showplace of northern Utah. It later deteriorated and was moved to the nearby community of Howell.

In 1902 the Southern Pacific Railroad, which had absorbed the Central Pacific, decided to shorten the line by building a trestle across Great Salt Lake. When finished in 1904, the Lucin Cutoff replaced the original line running north of the lake, although the Promontory line continued to be used occasionally when bad weather threatened the cutoff. Finally, in 1942, the company tore up the rails between Lucin and Corinne and contributed the scrap iron to the war effort. Amid ceremonies with two engines facing each other, workmen began the task by pulling up the 'last spike" at Promontory. ☐

Union Pacific

Promontory in late summer, 1869.

Golden Spike Vicinity

SCALE IN MILES

MARCH 1969

SIGNIFICANCE OF THE PACIFIC RAILROAD

With one exception the Pacific Railroad confirmed the expectations of its advocates and justified the participation of the U.S. Government. Politically, the Railroad Act of 1862 strengthened the loyal element in California, and undoubtedly insured (if insurance were needed) the continued allegiance of the Pacific Coast to the United States during the Civil War. Militarily, the railroad (more accurately, the railroad network that developed between 1869 and 1884) provided the key to conquering the Indians, and the means of considerably improving coastal defenses on the Pacific coast. It also furnished quicker and cheaper transportation for Government supplies and the mail. Commercially, it permitted a vast and profitable trade to develop between East and West. Only in the confident assurance of a huge trade with Asia—the principal motive—were the promoters of the Pacific Railroad disappointed. In November 1869, 6 months after the Golden Spike ceremony, the first ship steamed through the newly completed Suez Canal and destroyed this hope.

Aside from this contemporary significance, there was a larger and more profound significance which the projectors of the Pacific Railroad only dimly perceived. The Union Pacific and Central Pacific hastened the end of the continental frontier. They did not, as writers occasionally generalize, destroy the frontier. "From a narrow strip across the plains," said historian Frederick L. Paxson, "Indians had been pushed to one side and another and a single track had crossed the mountains, but north and south great areas remained untouched, for the demolition of the frontier had only just begun." Nevertheless, "In the history of the frontier the Union Pacific Railway marks the beginning of the end." The end did not come until after completion, in 1882-84, of the other transcontinental railroads, and then as a result of the collective influence of all. But the Central Pacific and Union Pacific established the process by which the end was attained.

This process had two stages. First, the railroad pierced the Indian barrier and gradually ate into it on either side of the right-of-way. Next it brought in its wake immigration, settlement, and development of industry and agriculture. The frontier inevitably disappeared. Settlement of the plains and mountains had been entirely unforeseen by the builders of the first Pacific Railroad, who wished only to bridge the "Great American Desert" and tap the commerce of Asia. But business from along the line came to furnish the bulk of traffic on the transcontinental railroads and tempered the disappointment over failure to capture the Asiatic trade.

Frederick Jackson Turner's famous frontier thesis, advanced in 1893, noted an essential difference between the Midwestern and Far Western frontiers of the United States and the determining role in this difference played by the railroad: "the frontier reached by the Pacific Railroad, surveyed into rectangles, guarded by the United States Army, and recruited by the daily immigrant ship, moved forward at a swifter pace and in a different way than the frontier reached by the birch canoe or the pack horse." Paxson, Turner's leading disciple, carried this thinking a step further: "The effort that finally destroyed the continental frontier differed from all earlier movements in the same direction in that it was self-conscious, deliberate, and national." After 40 years of controversy the principle of Federal aid to internal improvements at last gained general acceptance with passage of the Railroad Act of 1862. With this measure and later amendatory legislation, Congress struck the first really effective blow at the frontier. And while the first transcontinental railroad was under construction, Congress insured the complete collapse of the frontier by legislating aid to the Northern Pacific, Atlantic and Pacific, Texas and Pacific, and Southern Pacific railroads.

Thus the paramount historical significance of the first transcontinental railroad lies in its effect upon the Far Western frontier. It made the first serious and permanent breech in the frontier, and it established the process by which the entire frontier was to be demolished. ☐

Robert Weinstein Collection

A lone Indian gazes upon C.P. track in the Palisades section of the Humboldt River

Santa Fe Railway

A century after the joining of the rails at Promontory Summit, America's transcontinental railroads continue to foster the economic and political unity of the Nation. Sleek diesel liners hasten freight and passengers from Atlantic to Pacific in half the time of their wood-burning ancestors. Speeding across prairie and desert, or threading the passes of the Rockies and Sierra, they symbolize a dream come true beyond the most fanciful imaginings of the promoters and builders of the Pacific Railroad.

ADMINISTRATION Golden Spike National Historic Site is administered by the National Park Service, U.S. Department of the Interior. A superintendent, whose address is P.O. Box W, Brigham City, Utah 84302-0923, is in charge.

AMERICA'S NATURAL RESOURCES As the Nation's principal conservation agency, the Department of the Interior has basic responsibilities for water, fish, wildlife, mineral, land, park, and recreational resources. Indian and Territorial affairs are other major concerns of America's "Department of Natural Resources." The Department works to assure the wisest choice in managing all our resources so each will make its full contribution to a better United States—now and in the future.

HISTORICAL HANDBOOK SERIES NO. 40 This publication is one of a series of handbooks describing the historical and archeological areas in the National Park System administered by the National Park Service, U.S. Department of the Interior. It is printed by the Government Printing Office and can be purchased from the Superintendent of Documents, Washington, D.C. 20402.

Reprint 1989

U.S. Department of the Interior / National Park Service

☆ U.S. GOVERNMENT PRINTING OFFICE : 1989 O -230-069